I0435315

CONTENTS

ABSTRACT

Department of Homeland Security (DHS) faces many complex security challenges. Similar to the Department of Defense (DOD) before 1986, DHS components compete against one another for parochial benefits. This competition limits unity of effort and reduces both effectiveness and efficiency. DHS needs a mechanism to attain unity of effort through unity of command at the operational level. Can a DOD type Joint Task Force (JTF) structure provide the unity of command needed at DHS? This paper explores the application of a JTF to one of DHS's complex security issues, the Akwesasne Territory.

INTRODUCTION

Is the Department of Homeland Security (DHS) prepared to address the most complex security issues facing our nation? On March 3, 2003, the United States combined 22 agencies into a single entity: the Department of Homeland Security[1]. A reaction to the September 11, 2001 (9/11) attacks, this new department's primary mission was to unite the power of these legacy agencies in an effort to prevent a future terrorist attack on the United States.[2] Today, the agencies within this department continue to operate under separate chains of command with separate prerogatives, and priorities. Due to overlapping responsibilities, friction points within the separate commands reduce efficiency and hamper mission effectiveness.[3] Other law enforcement agencies outside of DHS at the local, state, tribal and federal levels, report to their own respective chains of command. To execute its primary mission of preventing the entry of terrorists or their weapons of mass destruction from entering the United States, DHS requires unity of effort with these other agencies.[4] A Department Of Defense (DOD) modeled DHS Joint Task Force (JTF) structure will efficiently address the most complex security issues facing the nation today.

---

[1] U.S. Department of Homeland Security, "Creation of the Department of Homeland Security," accessed 15 April 2013, http://www.dhs.gov/creation-department-homeland-security

[2] U.S. Department of Homeland Security, "Our Mission," accessed 15 April 2013, http://www.dhs.gov/our-mission

[3] Christopher J. Lamb and Edward Marks, "Chief of Mission Authority as a Model for National Security Integration," In *Institute for National Strategic Studies Strategic Perspectives No.2,* ed. Phillip C. Saunders, (Washington, DC: National Defense University Press, 2010), 5

[4] U.S. Department of Homeland Security, "Law Enforcement Partnerships," accessed 16 April 2013, http://www.dhs.gov/topic/law-enforcement-partnerships

BACKGROUND

This paper uses the Akwesasne Territory as an example of a complex security issue. This territory is located in between the state of New York and the Canadian provinces of Ontario and Quebec. The international border runs through the center of the territory.[5] For a more detailed explanation of the geographical and political environment, please see Annex A. The U.S. portion of the territory is the Saint Regis Mohawk Reservation while the Canadian portion is the Akwesasne Mohawk Reservation.[6] Several roads cross the international border, yet there are no ports of entry or other infrastructure on these roads controlling the entry or exit of people or vehicles.[7] The Canadian portion of the territory is located on an island and two peninsulas. There is no bridge to the peninsulas and can only be reached directly by boat from Canada. Therefore, the Royal Canadian Mounted Police (RCMP) does not regularly patrol this portion of the territory.[8] DHS and interagency partners are responsible for the U.S. section. However, due to an insular tribal culture that is hostile to outside influence, these agencies do little enforcement on the territory itself.[9] Because of its unique political and geographic features, this territory is a source of significant smuggling.[10] In 2010, the National Drug Intelligence Center reported that the Akwesasne reservation was the primary entry point for high potency marijuana and 3,4-MethyleneDioxy-n-MethylAmphetamine, (MDMA) known as Ecstasy bound for New York and New Jersey.[11]

---

[5] U.S. Department of Homeland Security, U.S. Customs and Border Protection, Office of Border Patrol, *Akwesasne Area Assessment, FY2007,* (Swanton, VT, 2007), 5

[6] ibid., 5

[7] ibid., 10

[8] ibid., 15

[9] ibid., 15

[10] Bree Spencer, "Akwesasne: A Complex Challenge to U.S. Northern Border Security," *The National Strategy Forum Review*, 20, No.3 (2011): 1, http://www.nationalstrategy.com/Portals/0/documents/Akwesasne.pdf

[11] U.S. Department of Homeland Security, U.S. Customs and Border Protection, Office of Border Patrol, *Massena Station Threat Assessment FY 2012,* (Massena, NY, 2012), 7

There are several law enforcement agencies arrayed against this complex situation. A standalone agency within DHS, the U.S. Coast Guard (USCG) is responsible for policing the U.S. portion of the Saint Lawrence River that separates the reservation from mainland Canada.[12] A second DHS agency, U.S. Customs and Border Protection (CBP) has two separate components responsible for the reservation. The U.S. Border Patrol (USBP) patrols the land and the water between official ports of entry.[13] The Office of Air and Marine (OAM) support DHS entities with helicopter, unmanned and fixed wing air surveillance.[14] Operating under Immigration and Customs Enforcement (ICE), the primary criminal investigators for DHS is Homeland Security Investigations (HSI). HSI conducts long-term investigations on human and contraband smuggling.[15] Outside DHS, the Department of Justice (DOJ) has two criminal investigation agencies that operate in this arena. The Drug Enforcement Administration (DEA) investigates violations of U.S. drug laws.[16] The Bureau of Alcohol, Tobacco and Firearms (ATF) oversees the U.S. laws on tobacco.[17] Finally, The Saint Regis Mohawk and Akwesasne Mohawk tribes each have their own separate police departments.[18] The RCMP and New York State Police also patrol the area around their respective sides of the Akwesasne Territory.[19]

---

[12] U.S. Coast Guard, "Missions," accessed 26 March 2013, http://www.uscg.mil/top/missions/
[13] U.S. Customs and Border Protection, "U.S. Border Patrol," accessed 25 March 2013, http//cbp.gov/xp/cgov/border_security/border_patrol/
[14] U.S. Customs and Border Protection, "About Air and Marine," accessed 25 March 2013, http://www.cbp.gov/xp/cgov/border_security/am/about_oam/
[15] U.S. Immigration and Customs Enforcement, "Homeland Security Investigations," accessed 27 March 2013, http://www.ice.gov/about/offices/homeland-security-investigations/
[16] U.S. Drug Enforcement Administration, "DEA Mission Statement," accessed 26 March 2013, http://www.justice.gov/dea/about/mission.shtml.
[17] U.S. Department of Justice Bureau of Alcohol, Tobacco, and Firearms, " Our Mission," accessed 02 April 2013, http://www.atf.gov/content/About/about-atf
[18] U.S. Department of Homeland Security, U.S. Customs and Border Protection, Office of Border Patrol, *Akwesasne Area Assessment, FY2007,* (Swanton, VT, 2007), 15
[19] ibid., 15

Each of these organizations has their own chains of command. At the tactical level, these agencies conduct service specific operations out of stations or sub offices while higher direction, administration and logistic support come from sectors or field offices. Thus, interagency friction develops due to overlapping federal responsibilities in interdicting or investigating the smuggling of aliens, narcotics, or tobacco leading to the question "who's in charge?"[20]

One major point of friction coming from the above-mentioned question involves deciding how to proceed after an initial arrest or seizure. Uniformed policing departments want to move immediately to prosecution and share any information developed from the seizure with partner agencies.[21] However, most criminal investigators do not share information. They keep it compartmentalized in case files for potential admissible evidence in a future criminal trial.[22] This procedure becomes a source of friction with uniformed policing agencies who want to quickly apply this information for crime prevention.[23]

To mitigate some of this friction, agencies interact with each other through memorandums of understanding, councils, forums or working groups.[24] Task Forces (TF) developed from these forums share information and conduct joint investigations at the tactical level. Only the agents or officers detailed to the TF report to the TF commander.

---

[20]Michael D. Kennedy, "Securing the U.S. Southern Land Border: Enhancing the Interagency Effort," (strategy research project, U.S. Army War College, Carlisle Barracks, PA, 2011), 11 accessed 10 April 2013. http://www.dtic.mil/cgi-bin/GetTRDoc?AD=ADA543691

[21] Alan D. Bersin, "Lines and Flows: The Beginning and End of Borders," *Brooklyn Journal of International* Law 37, no.2 (2012), 400, http://connection.ebscohost.com/c/articles/76745671/lines-flows-beginning-end-borders

[22] ibid., 400

[23] ibid., 400

[24] Office of Inspector General, Department of Homeland Security, *DHS's Progress In Assessing Coordination Challenges Between Customs and Border Protection and Immigration and Customs Enforcement,* (Washington, DC:OIG, DHS, 2007), 13

The TF commander reports to his service organization. One example that operates on the Akwesasne is HSI's Border Enforcement Security Team (BEST).[25]

The disadvantage of this system is that it is staff centric. By having forums of equal ranked heads of agencies providing direction to a tactical unit, consensus becomes more important than effectiveness.[26] Furthermore, these forums only control a small number of forces, those on the TFs. To meet their service centric prerogatives, these agencies continue to direct the majority of their forces from the strategic and operational levels to the tactical level. There is no single commander, or staff organization tasked to assess the entire Akwesasne situation at the operational level with the authority to direct department wide capabilities in a joint fashion to rectify the security situation. Nor is there a single commander that directly reports to the DHS Secretary to influence inter-department unity of effort to address the issues on the Akwesasne. This lack of unity of command to achieve unity of effort reduces mission effectiveness. In 2010, the National Drug Intelligence Center estimated smugglers transported 13 tons of marijuana through the reservation every week.[27] The current agency-centric command structures have not addressed the complex security situation on the Akwesasne reservation.

[25] U.S. Immigration and Customs Enforcement, "Border Security Enforcement Task Force," accessed 26 March 2013, http://www.ice.gov/best/

[26] James L. Locher III, "Has it Worked? The Goldwater-Nichols Reorganization Act," *Naval War College Review* LIV, No. 4 (2001), 97

[27]U.S. Department of Homeland Security, U.S. Customs and Border Protection, Office of Border Patrol, *Massena Station Threat Assessment FY 2012*, (Massena, NY, 2012), 7

JOINT TASK FORCE (JTF)

This situation is similar to what the DOD faced before enactment of the Goldwater-Nichols Act. For a more detailed explanation, please see Annex B. Recalling the congressional legislation that mandated a command centric joint structure, prior Secretary of Defense Donald Rumsfeld commented on the inter agency lack of joint capability. "[It is] stove piped much like the four services were 20 years ago…[should ask the agencies to] give up some of their existing turf and authority in exchange for a stronger, faster, more efficient…joint effort."[28] DOD has seen mission performance improve by expanding commander centric leadership from the tactical level into the joint operational and strategic levels. "Historical analysis shows that commander-centric organizations outperform staff [or agency] centric, process-orientated organizations."[29] One reason for this performance is the ability to achieve quickly unity of effort. "[T]he highest degree of effectiveness is ensured by having unity of effort through unity of command."[30] In the past, not having unity of effort has resulted in numerous disasters; therefore, an organization must achieve it as quickly and effectively as possible.[31] In DOD, at the operational level, Joint Force Commander (JFC) who is in charge of a JTF embodies command centric leadership.

---

[28] Donald Rumsfeld, "9/11 Commission Report, 2004" , quoted in Christopher J. Lamb and Edward Marks, "Chief of Mission Authority as a Model for National Security Integration," In *Institute for National Strategic Studies Strategic Perspectives No.2,* ed. Phillip C. Saunders, (Washington, DC: National Defense University Press, 2010), vi

[29] Chairman, U.S. Joint Chiefs of Staff, *Joint Operations*, Joint Publication (JP) 3-0 (Washington, DC: CJCS, 11 August 2011), 11-1

[30] Milan Vego, *Joint Operational Warfare Theory and Practice*, (Newport, RI: U.S. Naval War College, 2007), VIII-13

[31] ibid., VIII-14

One of the concepts the JFC and his staff on the JTF's use is Operational Art. "Operational Art is the use of creative thinking by commanders and staff to design strategies, campaigns, major operations to organize and employ military forces."[32] Part of Operational Art is framing the situation using time, space, and force as factors. The JFC and his staff plan actions to balance these factors to increase the likelihood of successfully completing the mission. Using the time, space, and force framework, the Akwesasne situation and the other advantages of JTF applied to reduce the security gaps and improve efficiency.

TIME

One advantage a JTF can provide balancing the factor of time is planning for a long contest. In consultation with the DHS Secretary for strategic objectives, the JFC can describe the character of the situation. It will be long in duration, years rather than months and unlike a military operation, without a definitive end. From this understanding, the secretary can develop realistic strategic objectives. From these, the JFC with his staff can develop achievable operational objectives and metrics to track progress to meet the strategic objectives. This provides data to manage expectations within both DHS and external partners at the local, state, tribal, federal, and international level. An example would be the U.S. Congress in its oversight role. By developing realistic timeframes and objectives, the JTF builds credibility with its chain of command and external partners.

---

[32] Chairman, U.S. Joint Chiefs of Staff, *Joint Operations*, Joint Publication (JP) 3-0 (Washington, DC: CJCS, 11 August 2011), 11-3

A second advantage of a JTF balancing the factor of time is the ability to plan sequels for expected events and branches for unexpected events. By planning concurrently rather than sequentially, the forces maintain a high operational tempo reducing the time the opponent has to react.[33] Using his J5 staff, the JFC can have sequel or branch plans for shifts in the smuggling patterns or tactics. As the higher operational and adaptive tempo places more local smuggling organizations on "death ground"[34] the J5 can plan branches and sequels for increases in violence against law enforcement and methods to respond to such incidents. With some of the militant Native American Indian groups allied with the smugglers, the J5 can also develop branch plans for unrest in the community sparked by the arrests of local smugglers. By having plans prepared before events occur, the J5 provides appropriate options to the JFC. Without having to develop options while events occur, the JFC can make better decisions that can result in successful resolutions to several possible high profile events.

A third advantage of a JTF structure is the flexible nature of the structure that is superior to other organizational systems in balancing time. Just as with a DOD JTF, the DHS Secretary can stand it down once its mission is complete or reassign it to a different mission. It is designed to have a simple chain of command and is not responsible for administration or logistics, which will remain with the agencies.[35] It will integrate the capabilities needed, not to represent or command every component of the department. As an example, this proposed JTF does not integrate the CBP Office of Field Operations, as its port of entry operations are outside of the reservation and are not part of the security situation.

---

[33] Milan Vego, *Joint Operational Warfare Theory and Practice*, (Newport, RI: U.S. Naval War College, 2007), VIII-13
[34] Tzu, Sun, *The Art of War*, ed. and trans, by Samuel B. Griffith, (London UK: Oxford University Press, 1963), 131
[35] Milan Vego, *Joint Operational Warfare Theory and Practice*, (Newport, RI: U.S. Naval War College, 2007), VIII-11

It can function for weeks or years, depending on the task to complete. This will prevent the tendency of a creating another layer of permanent bureaucracy which can reduce efficiency and fail to balance the factor of time.

Two other models exist in the interagency that do not balance the factor of time as a JTF does. The first is the National Incident Management System (NIMS).[36] Mandated under Homeland Security Presidential Directive-5, NIMS is the structure for the interagency to use when addressing a specific incident.[37] An example would be a natural disaster or a National Special Security Event such as the Super Bowl. A key concept of NIMS is unified command, a staff centric process where agency representatives provide joint management direction to a single incident commander.[38] As previously described, this type of system does not achieve unity of effort quickly, reducing the ability of this structure to balance the factor of time.

The second organizational structure that does not balance time as well as a JTF is a regional system. Prior to 9/11, the defunct Immigration and Naturalization Service and Customs Service both employed regional systems.[39] Similar to a Geographic Combat Command, these regions exercised command and control over multi-service sub components. This system led to regional commissioners who ran their areas differently and competed against each other for resources.[40]

---

[36] Federal Emergency Management Agency, "NIMS Overview Presentation," accessed 15 April 2013, http://www.fema.gov/library/viewRecord.do?id=6449
[37] ibid.
[38] ibid.
[39] Michael D. Kennedy, "Securing the U.S. Southern Land Border: Enhancing the Interagency Effort," Strategy research project, (U.S. Army War College, Carlisle Barracks, PA, 2011), 21 accessed 10 April 2013. http://www.dtic.mil/cgi-bin/GetTRDoc?AD=ADA543691
[40] ibid., 21

Without a position or organization similar to the DOD Chairman of the Joint Chiefs of Staff (CJCS) and Joint Staff to referee amongst the regions, inconsistent procedures and problems in allocating resources arose. Strong regional commissioners would not give up resources to weaker commissioners trying addressing their threats.[41] DHS disbanded the regions in 2003. In 2011, in response to a large amount of illegal activity, CBP stood up a regional structure, Joint Field Command-Arizona.[42] This organization is responsible for not just a single task but for all of CBP missions including border security and trade facilitation. It is also responsible for the logistics of the sub components within the command.[43] Unlike a JTF, this command widely focused on the whole CBP mission rather than a specific task. It also does not include ICE HSI forces that are essential to addressing the security situation in Arizona. A JTF structure provides a flexible model to fit the circumstances of the situation, quickly gain unity of effort, establish reasonable objectives, plan concurrently to achieve higher tempo, and not create another permanent bureaucracy. All of these benefits balance the factor of time.

SPACE

The second operational factor is space. One consideration of space is the characteristics of the physical environment. To balance this operational factor, the JFC and his staff must be familiar with these characteristics of the space in question, as it will affect the deployment of forces.

---

[41] ibid., 22
[42] U.S. Customs and Border Protection, "Joint Field Command Arizona," accessed 26 March 2013, http://www.cbp.gov/xp/cgov/border_security/arizona/
[43] ibid.

One example is the Saint Laurence River and its tributaries that separate the Canadian portion of the reservation from the rest of country. In the summer, these rivers are free flowing with varying depths depending on hydroelectric generation and shipping needs.[44] Due to these characteristics, smugglers use customized vessels equipped to operate at high speeds and in shallow depths to transport narcotics or people onto the reservation from Canada. In the winter, the river turns to ice and once it is thick enough, the Akwesasne residents establish roads over it.[45] These environmental characteristics inhibit interdictions on the Saint Lawrence River before the contraband reaches the Akwesasne using standard vessels and equipment. Understanding these tactical considerations, a JFC can request through the DHS Secretary for the USCG, USBP and OAM to provide a capability to operate in this unique seasonal environment. The JFC can also request from the interagency to provide an existing capability to overcome these features. For example, DOD riverine units with USBP agents on board could perform law enforcement interdictions. These units can fill the gap while the DHS components develop an organic capability.

A second consideration of space is that of human space. Human space includes factors such as government, ethnicity, traditions, and culture. Here are some ways a JTF can have an impact on the human space. First, with the Akwesasne the JFC and his staff can establish relationships with various tribal governments within the Akwesasne Territory. Using his direct line to the DHS Secretary, the JTF can quickly provide both homeland security grants and coordinate with the interagency to provide other development grants for the tribal governments.

---

[44] U.S. Department of Homeland Security, U.S. Customs and Border Protection, Office of Border Patrol, *Akwesasne Area Assessment, FY2007,* (Swanton, VT, 2007), 7
[45] ibid., 7

These grants can build the capacity of the government to provide opportunities to employ their people legally without them having to resort to smuggling. The JFC can also empower the tribe to address smuggling issues using its own police force. With agreement from the DHS Secretary, the JFC can delegate authorities to the Saint Regis Mohawk Tribal Police Department (SRMTPD) to enforce laws against smuggling. The Bureau of Indian Affairs has already designated SRMTPD personnel as federal officers.[46]

Second, with the assistance of DOJ, the JFC and his staff can establish relationships with the DEA and ATF to attain unity of effort on enforcement actions and intelligence sharing on the territory. With their responsibilities over narcotics and tobacco respectively, the DEA and ATF have critical capabilities needed for JTF to complete its mission. The DEA conducts drug investigations in the cities that are the destination for the contraband smuggled south through the Akwesasne reservation. With the intelligence from ongoing DEA investigations linked to Akwesasne based smugglers, the JTF's J2 staff can identify trends and targets on which the J3 staff may focus their operations. Through regulation and investigation, the ATF can influence illegal cigarette smuggling going into Canada by focusing on the Akwesasne cigarette producers. Information from these investigations can identify subjects smuggling cigarettes north and contraband south. If any friction arises from the DOJ agencies that jeopardize the unity of effort to reduce smuggling on the Akwesasne, the JFC can report this conflict to the DHS secretary to be resolved at the department level between the Secretary and Attorney General.

---

[46] Richard S.Hartunian, "Oneida Nation Police Department and Saint Regis Mohawk Police Officers Awarded Bureau of Indian Affairs Federal Officer Certifications," Department of Justice, United States Attorney, Northern District of New York. 15 June 2012, http://www.justice.gov/usao/nyn/news/1671-3290-831307008.pdf

Finally, coordinating with the Department of State, the JFC and his staff can establish a positive working relationship with Canadian officials to gain access to the Canadian portion of the reservation. After demonstrating progress on reducing cigarette smuggling, the JFC can request Canada to empower U.S. and SRMTPD officers to enforce Canadian federal law on the Akwesasne Reservation and the surrounding waters.[47] In turn, the U.S. would designate Akwesasne Mohawk Reservation police officers to enforce federal laws in the U.S. portion of the reservation. This concept already exists in the Beyond the Borders Framework. It is utilized it the ship-rider program where Canadian and U.S. federal officers enforce each other's laws on international waters such as the Great Lakes.[48] With this type of agreement, the JTF will have a force to execute missions in previously inaccessible portions of the reservation.

FORCE

Applying the previously mentioned concepts of unity of command, and those described in time, and space, a JTF can apply an optimized force to the Akwesasne situation in the following manner. Using a multilayered approach, the JTF's first layer would be DHS high-speed shallow draft vessels with U.S. and Canadian cross-designated federal authority crews to intercept smuggling on the Saint Lawrence River. In the winter, the same crews could be used to pilot over ice airboats.

---

[47] Stefanie Von Hlatky, "The Rhetoric and Reality of Border Policy Coordination Between Canada and the U.S.," *International Journal* 67, No. 2 (2012), 441 http://internationaljournal.ca/post/26182981113/volume-67-issue-2-a-new-agenda-for-peace
[48] U.S. Department of Homeland Security, "Beyond the Border: A Shared Vision for Perimeter Security and Economic Competiveness Action Plan." accessed 03 April 2013, 21, http://www.dhs.gov/beyond-border-shared-vision-perimeter-security-and-economic-competitiveness.

The second layer would consist of Saint Regis and Akwesasne police units with U.S. and Canadian federal authorities to interdict or investigate smuggling on the entire Akwesasne reservation. A third layer would consist of DHS agents and cooperating state and local officers interdicting smuggling outside the reservation. In each of these layers, DHS and interagency aircraft would provide responsible agents responsible with targeting and imagery support for interdictions.

Finally, after each seizure the JFC could decide to proceed with a long-term criminal investigation to dismantle an overarching criminal organization beyond the reservation or short-term investigation to dismantle any smuggling cells operating on the reservation. The JTF would exchange information from these seizures and investigations with the interagency to develop timely situational awareness to plan for future operations.

COUNTER ARGUMENT

A counter to the preceding analysis is that DHS could not implement a JTF structure today as the situation is not ripe for such a change. Even after multiple examples of harmful inter service rivalry during World War II; it took the failures in Operations Eagle Claw, the Iranian hostage rescue attempt and Urgent Fury, the Invasion of Grenada to convince the U.S. Congress to force a joint military through the Goldwater Nichols Act.[49] After 9/11, Congress formed DHS over the objections of then President Bush.[50]

---

[49]James L. Locher III, "Has it Worked? The Goldwater-Nichols Reorganization Act," *Naval War College Review* LIV, No. 4 (2001), 100
[50] Washington Post, Politics, "Homeland Security Department," accessed 30, March 2013,http://www.washingtonpost.com/politics/homeland-securitydepartment/gIQALxPx4O _topic.html

Even with this sense to promote unity among the various federal law enforcement components, the FBI, DEA, and ATF remained in DOJ. To remain independent, the agencies within and outside of DHS now cooperate to the point that limits the calls for further integration.[51] Furthermore, the U.S. does not know of any terrorist organizations operate or use the Akwesasne area. Compounded by calls for budget austerity, a JTF structure is not needed, desired, or affordable.

REBUTTAL

The U.S. must not wait for terrorist organizations to act. It must act in a disciplined fashion, harnessing existing forces and expends funds frugally. These organizations have shown the ability to adapt and seek new vulnerabilities as avenues to attack the United States. These organizations could discover and exploit vulnerabilities such as the Akwesasne as an entry points into the U.S. A JTF can close these vulnerabilities more efficiently than the existing structures by shifting the responsibility from multiple cooperating DHS agencies with national objectives to a commander with a single objective. Following DOD doctrine on basing JTFs on existing commands, DHS can also reduce costs by using existing federal facilities and personnel from the DHS components.

---

[51] Christopher J. Lamb and Edward Marks, "Chief of Mission Authority as a Model for National Security Integration," In *Institute for National Strategic Studies Strategic Perspectives No.2*, ed. Phillip C. Saunders, (Washington, DC: National Defense University Press, 2010), 10

RECOMMENDATIONS

DHS should first establish a JTF structure. To accomplish this, DHS should submit draft language to the U.S. Congress that describes the authorities of the JFC, and place them in U.S. Code.[52] This draft must describe the structure of command with the JFC reporting to the DHS Secretary. It must also describe the role of the DHS components switching from an operational mission to an administrative mission once their forces fall under a JTF. This will provide the JFC sufficient authority to the commander to complete his or her task.

Second, DHS must identify locations for JTF deployment such as the Akwesasne Territory. Other possible areas are South Texas and Arizona. DHS must provide funds to the JFC commanders to establish small headquarters and staff in these locations. From the DHS secretary's strategic objectives, the JFCs and their staff will develop operational objectives and metrics to assess the task of securing these complex areas.

Specifically for the Akwesasne, DHS should establish a high-level workgroup that includes DOJ, DOS, and Canadian officials. This group can develop the existing Ship-rider concept in the Beyond the Borders framework into a joint Akwesasne Tribal Police force, which can operate on both sides of the border within the territory. This will enable the prosecution of violators utilizing the applicable Canadian or U.S. federal laws depending on the location of the crime.

---

[52] ibid., 18

Finally, if there is no complex security issue, DHS should use existing command structures rather than using a JTF. DOD deigned the JTF structure to complete a specific task at the operational level, not to act as a permanent regional command. If DHS wants to expand joint organization to the theater level in areas without complex security issues, consider regions based on DOD GCC model. However, DHS will need to develop structures similar to DOD CJCS, and Joint Staff, to moderate these regions to avoid previously described past mistakes.

CONCLUSION

The Akwesasne area is a complex and dynamic security issue with weaknesses that are vulnerable to the exploits of smuggling operations and terrorist organizations. Given the damage a few motivated individuals can inflict, The U.S. must close all security gaps. Without unity of command, the forces currently responsible for securing the Akwesasne see each other as rivals and work in isolation, limiting their ability to close these gaps. This situation mirrors what the DOD faced prior to1986 when Congress mandated a Joint Force Command structure to overcome inter service rivalries. Using a JTF structure with a JFC, DHS can implement the lessons learned from DOD. Applying unity of command and Operational Art with all DHS forces, a JTF structure would address complex security situations such as the Akwesasne Territory and close the gaps in America's security.

ANNEX A

AKWESASNE

Located at the confluence of the Saint Lawrence and Saint Regis Rivers, the territory known as the Akwesasne translates to "the land where the partridge drums"[53]. Part of the six nation Iroquois Confederacy, the Mohawk tribe began permanent settlement of the Akwesasne around 1750 from Kahnawake, near present day Montreal[54]. At the conclusion of the War of American Revolution, the U.S. and Britain ratified the Treaty of Paris in 1783. This document determined the boundary between America and the then British controlled Canada. Under Article 2(d) of the treaty, the international boundary began at the source of the Saint Croix River, now located in the center of Maine.[55] This border then followed a line starting at the 45th parallel of northern latitude until it intersected the Saint Lawrence River in upper New York State.[56] Later, in 1794 the "Jay Treaty" between the U.S. and England gave Native American Indians (NAI) born in both the U.S. and Canada the right to cross the border freely.[57] Unlike like the experience of many other tribes, the Mohawks on the Akwesasne never went to war against the U.S. or faced forced eviction from their land. The Mohawks on the Akwesasne established a formal relationship with New York State in 1802 and with Canada in 1899.[58] U.S. federal tribal recognition occurred in the early 1970s.[59]

---

[53] Akwesasne.ca, "Akwesasne: Land Where the Partridge Drums," accessed 02 April 2013. http://akwesasne.ca/history.html

[54] Aren Akwes, *St. Regis Akwesasne Mohawks*. (Hogansburg, NY: Akwesasne Counselor Organization, 1948), 6

[55] Treaty of Paris, Article 2, Section.D, accessed 04 April 2013 http://www.ourdocuments.gov/doc.php?flash=true&doc=6

[56] Matthew Farfan, *The 45th Parallel Border and its Problems, The Vermont Quebec Border Life on the Line*, (Charlestown SC: Acadia Publishing, 2009), 6

[57] Joshua J Tonra, "The Threat of Border Security on Indigenous Free Passage Rights in North America," *Syracuse Journal of Law and International Law and Commerce*, 34, No.1 (2006), 223 http://connection.ebscohost.com/c/articles/24840712/threat-border-security-indigenous-free-passage-rights-north-america.

[58] Aren Akwes, *St. Regis Akwesasne Mohawks*, (Hogansburg, NY: Akwesasne Counselor Organization, 1948), 15

[59] Saint Regis Mohawk Tribe, "Culture and History," accessed 20 April 2013, http://www.srmt-nsn.gov/government/culture_and_history/

With the right of free passage confirmed by treaty, Akwesasne NAI crossed the border daily through several roads established on the territory or across the Saint Lawrence River by boat.

Due its location on the border, the smuggling of people and contraband has always occurred on the reservation. [60] Although significant federal enforcement occurred for a time during prohibition, prior to 9/11 the number of agents assigned to this area was low.[61] In the 1980's, due to high taxes on tobacco products in Canada, cigarette manufacturing and smuggling began on the Saint Regis Mohawk Reservation. [62] These cigarettes were smuggled north using boats through the Akwesasne Mohawk Reservation into mainland Canada. Smuggling activity increased further with the rise in popularity of high potency hydroponically grown marijuana and MDMA. Criminal enterprises in Canada manufacture these substances in large quantities.[63] These narcotics began to be smuggled south into the U.S. The smuggling of people continued to occur with these increases in contraband smuggling. These people would blend in with the local traffic exiting the Akwesasne Mohawk Reservation into the Saint Regis Mohawk Reservation.

After 9/11, the U.S. began to enforce its border controls rigorously and provided additional agents.[64] Not only did U.S. law enforcement target contraband smuggling, with the concern of terrorists entering, human smuggling took on new importance.

---

[60] Bree Spencer, "Akwesasne: A Complex Challenge to U.S. Northern Border Security," *The National Strategy Forum Review*, 20, no.3 (2011), 1, http://www.nationalstrategy.com/Portals/0/documents/Akwesasne.pdf

[61] Darren Bonaparte, "The History of Akwesasne from Pre-Contact to Modern Times," accessed 10 April 2013, http://www.wampumchronicles.com/history.html

[62] ibid.,

[63] Office of National Drug Control Policy, *National Northern Border Counternarcotics Strategy*, (Washington, DC: Executive Office of the President of the United States, January 2012), 4

[64] Wilson Ring, "Post- 9/11Security Divides Life on the Northern Border," Associated Press. 13 August 2011, accessed 20 April 2013. http://news.yahoo.com/post-9-11-security-divides-life-northern-border-172655474.html

Although NAIs are free to cross the border, the U.S. has the responsibility to examine all people entering to ensure they are NAI and entitled to this right.[65] However, after decades of not enforcing this mandate, enforcement is problematic. The network of roads crossing the border and the amount of local traffic on them make examination of all those entering impossible. Furthermore, the local community not involved in smuggling resent having their rights restricted through examination. The residents are hostile during vehicle stops or turn around and reenter the Canadian portion, which U.S. officers cannot enter.

Today, the area is divided physically and politically into four sections. Cornwall Island is within the Saint Lawrence River in Ontario, Canada. The peninsulas of Saint Regis Village and the Snye are located in Quebec Canada. The U.S. section begins on the landside of Saint Regis Village and the Snye in the state of New York. The Saint Regis Mohawk Tribe governs the U.S. portion while the Akwesasne Mohawk Tribe governs the Canadian portion. Each use a number of chiefs elected to three-year terms.[66] There is a third government, the Mohawk National Council of Chiefs (MNCC). It is the traditional form of government with three clan mothers appointing chiefs for life terms. Neither the United States nor Canada recognize the MNCC, however it has popular support.[67]

A fourth organization on the Akwesasne Territory claims to speak for the residents, the Warrior Society. Organized in its current form in 1972 at Kahnawake, Quebec, it represents the Iroquois Confederacy and advocates for Native American sovereignty.[68] This organization has some members who are militant or allied with smugglers.

---

[65] Joshua J Tonra, "The Threat of Border Security on Indigenous Free Passage Rights in North America," *Syracuse Journal of Law and International Law and Commerce*, 34, no.1 (2006), 222
[66] ibid., 18
[67] ibid., 18
[68] Haudenosaunee,"National Defense and Public Security," accessed 10 April 2013, http://www.kahnawakelonghouse.com/index.php?mid=1&p=3.

This organization has both supported the MNCC and the elected chiefs at different times. The Warrior Society will at times arrive at the site of law enforcement actions in an attempt to intimidate or incite the officers.[69] With the unique location of the border dividing a proud insular community, it creates a complex security situation for DHS.

---

[69] U.S. Department of Homeland Security, U.S. Customs and Border Protection, Office of Border Patrol, *Akwesasne Area Assessment, FY2007*, (Swanton, VT, 2007), 33

ANNEX B

JOINT TASK FORCES

The first mention of Task Forces (TF) in the United States is in 1921 in U.S. Navy General Order 30. [70] It described a force containing required elements of the type-organized fleet to complete a specific task. During World War II, the Navy saw the flexibility advantages of task forces. When the need arose, the fleet commander assembled the required force to execute a task and once completed he could be retained or disbanded it.[71] Furthermore, the TF commander did not have to concern himself with administration of the ships just on executing the mission. The ship type commanders would be responsible for administration, training, and equipping the specific ships, such as the destroyer force or the carrier force.[72] This system worked well when used within one service department; however, this was not the case when two services were involved.

The U.S. military services had a tradition of inter-service rivalry. The competition over resources and methods of force employment created this rivalry.[73] U.S. Congress members further increased this competition, pitting the services against each other for projects within their districts or states.[74] Due to all the wasted effort created by this rivalry during the war, President Truman reorganized the services into the Department of Defense.[75]

---

[70] Julius Augustus Furer, *Administration of the Navy Department in World War II,* (Washington DC: United States Printing Office, 1959), 174

[71] ibid., 174

[72] ibid., 175

[73] James L. Locher III, "Has it Worked? The Goldwater-Nichols Reorganization Act," *Naval War College Review* LIV, No. 4 (2001), 95

[74] ibid., 98

[75] ibid., 98

However, to satisfy both the services and members of congress, the individual services remained the most powerful within the organization.[76]

This situation continued until two high profile incidents, the failed rescue attempt of the Iranian hostages, known as Operation Eagle Claw and the invasion of Grenada also known as Operation Urgent Fury.[77] Although the, the services were using the term JTF in these operations and appointing an overall commander, true command authority only existed with each service commander. Few of the personnel had operated with other services before commencing the operations.[78] Furthermore, there was no joint staff or doctrine to properly plan for these missions. In 1986, Congress passed the Goldwater-Nichols Act to rectify this situation, establishing a joint force commander, a joint staff, creation of joint doctrine, and joint training.[79]

A key aspect of the legislation was removing the service chiefs from operational command. Instead, Geographic Combat Commanders (GCCs) would be responsible for mission execution at the strategic level.[80] Reporting directly to the Secretary of Defense (SECDEF), these GCCs appoint a Joint Force Commander to a JTF to execute the mission at the operational level.[81] A JTF will have staff organized into several sections including intelligence (J2), operations (J3) and plans (J5) to support the JFC.[82]

---

[76] ibid., 99
[77] ibid., 100
[78] ibid., 100
[79] ibid., 99
[80] Chairman, U.S. Joint Chiefs of Staff, *Doctrine for the Armed Forces of the United States* (JP) 1 (Washington, DC: CJCS, 20 March 2009), xiv
[81] ibid., xxvi
[82] ibid., V-15

Through the GCC and SECDEF, the JFC and his staff request required service capabilities to apply jointly to complete the JTF's task. The short chain of command from the JFC through the GCC to the SECDEF also provides high-level de-confliction with other U.S. agencies.[83] This ensures unity of effort to apply all sources of U.S. power needed to complete the mission: Diplomacy, Information, Military and Economic (DIME).[84] Although it is not a perfect system, inter service rivalry has diminished and the successful execution of missions using joint forces has increased.[85]

---

[83] ibid., xx

[84] ibid., x

[85] James L. Locher III, "Has it Worked? The Goldwater-Nichols Reorganization Act," *Naval War College Review* LIV, No. 4 (2001), 110

AKWESASNE TERRITORY MAP

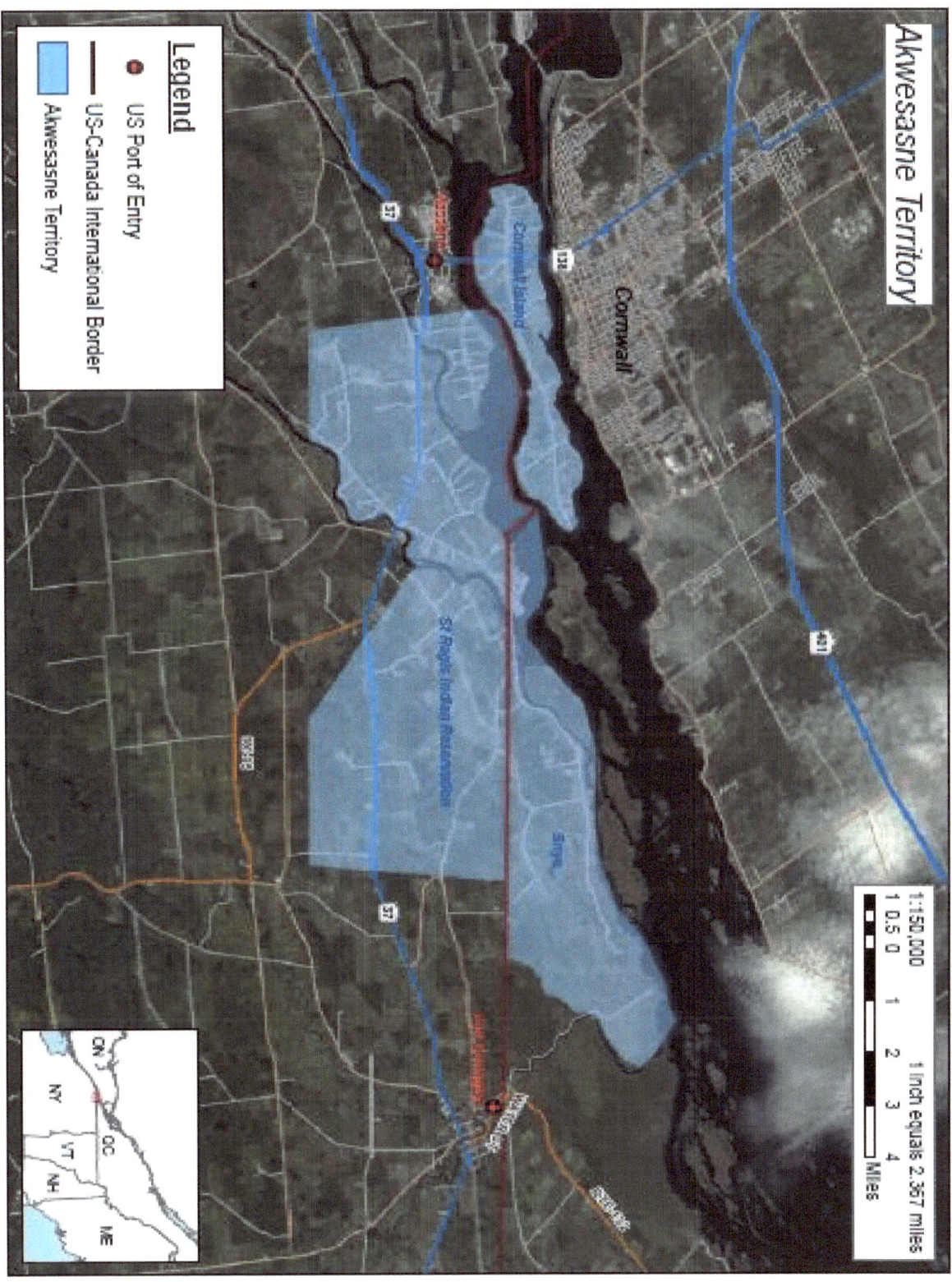

Map Source: U.S. Department of Homeland Security, U.S. Customs and Border Protection, Office of Border Patrol, *Akwesasne Area Assessment, FY2007*, (Swanton, VT, 2007), 7

BIBLIOGRAPHY

Akweks, Aren. *St. Regis Akwesasne Mohawks.* Hogansburg, NY: Akwesasne Counselor Organization, 1948.

Akwesasne.ca. "Akwesasne: Land Where the Partridge Drums." Accessed 02 April 2013. http://akwesasne.ca/history.html.

Bersin, Alan D. "Lines and Flows: The Beginning and End of Borders." *Brooklyn Journal of International Law* 37, No.2 (2012) 389-406. http://connection.ebscohost.com/c/articles/76745671/lines-flows-beginning-end-borders.

Bonaparte, Darren. "The History of Akwesasne From Pre-Contact to Modern Times." Accessed 10 April 2013. http://www.wampumchronicles.com/history.html

Farfan, Matthew. *The 45th Parallel Border and its Problems, The Vermont Quebec Border Life on the Line.* Charlestown SC: Acadia Publishing, 2009.

Federal Emergency Management Agency. "NIMS Overview Presentation." Accessed 15 April 2013. http://www.fema.gov/library/viewRecord.do?id=6449.

Furer, Julius Augustus. *Administration of the Navy Department in World War II.* Washington DC: United States Printing Office, 1959.

Hartunian, Richard S. "Oneida Nation Police Department and Saint Regis Mohawk Police Officers Awarded Bureau of Indian Affairs Federal Officer Certifications." Department of Justice, United States Attorney, Northern District of New York. 15 June 2012. http://www.justice.gov/usao/nyn/news/1671-3290-831307008.pdf.

Haudenosaunee. "National Defense and Public Security." Accessed 10 April 2013. http://www.kahnawakelonghouse.com/index.php?mid=1&p=3.

Kennedy, Michael D. "Securing the U.S. Southern Land Border: Enhancing the Interagency Effort." Strategy research project, U.S. Army War College, Carlisle Barracks, PA., 2011. Accessed 10 April 2013. http://www.dtic.mil/cgi-bin/GetTRDoc?AD=ADA543691

Lamb, Christopher J., and Marks, Edward. "Chief of Mission Authority as a Model for National Security Integration." In *Institute for National Strategic Studies Strategic Perspectives No.2.* Edited by Phillip C. Saunders. Washington, DC: National Defense University Press, 2010.

Locher, James L., III. "Has it Worked? The Goldwater-Nichols Reorganization Act." *Naval War College Review.* LIV, No. 4 (2001) 95-115.

Office of Inspector General, Department of Homeland Security. *DHS's Progress In Assessing Coordination Challenges Between Customs and Border Protection and Immigration and Customs Enforcement.* Washington, DC: OIG, DHS, 2007.

Office of National Drug Control Policy. *National Northern Border Counternarcotics Strategy.* Washington, DC: Executive Office of the President of the United States, January 2012.

Ring, Wilson. "Post- 9/11Security Divides Life on the Northern Border." *Associated Press.* 13 August 2011. Accessed 20 April 2013. http://news.yahoo.com/post-9-11-security-divides-life-northern-border-172655474.html.

Rumsfeld, Donald. "9/11 Commission Report, 2004." quoted in Christopher J. Lamb and Edward Marks. "Chief of Mission Authority as a Model for National Security Integration," in *Institute for National Strategic Studies Strategic Perspectives No.2*, Edited by Phillip C. Saunders. Washington, DC: National Defense University Press, 2010.

Saint Regis Mohawk Tribe. "Culture and History." Accessed 20 April 2013. http://www.srmt-nsn.gov/government/culture_and_history/

Spencer, Bree. "Akwesasne: A Complex Challenge to U.S. Northern Border Security." *The National Strategy Forum Review.* 20, No.3 (2011). http://www.nationalstrategy.com/Portals/0/documents/Akwesasne.pdf.

Sun, Tzu. *The Art of War.* Edited and translated by Samuel B. Griffith, London, UK: Oxford University Press, 1963.

Treaty of Paris, Article 2, Section D. Accessed 04 April 2013. http://www.ourdocuments.gov/doc.php?flash=true&doc=6.

Tonra, Joshua J. "The Threat of Border Security on Indigenous Free Passage Rights in North America." *Syracuse Journal of Law and International Law and Commerce.* 34, No.1 (2006) 221-257 http://connection.ebscohost.com/c/articles/24840712/threat-border-security-indigenous-free-passage-rights-north-america.

U.S. Coast Guard. "Missions." Accessed 26 March 2013. http://www.uscg.mil/top/missions/.

U.S. Customs and Border Protection. "About Air and Marine." Accessed 25 March 2013. http://www.cbp.gov/xp/cgov/border_security/am/about_oam/.

U.S. Customs and Border Protection. "Joint Field Command Arizona." Accessed 26 March 2013. http://www.cbp.gov/xp/cgov/border_security/arizona/.

U.S. Customs and Border Protection. "U.S. Border Patrol." Accessed 25 March 2013. http://www.cbp.gov/xp/cgov/border_security/border_patrol/.

U.S. Department of Homeland Security. "Beyond the Border: A Shared Vision for Perimeter Security and Economic Competiveness Action Plan." Accessed 03 April 2013. http://www.dhs.gov/beyond-border-shared-vision-perimeter-security-and-economic-competitiveness.

U.S. Department of Homeland Security. "Creation of the Department of Homeland Security." Accessed 15 April 2013. http://www.dhs.gov/creation-department-homeland-security.

U.S. Department of Homeland Security. "Law Enforcement Partnerships." Accessed 16 April 2013. http://www.dhs.gov/topic/law-enforcement-partnerships.

U.S. Department of Homeland Security. "Our Mission." Accessed 15 April 2013. http://www.dhs.gov/our-mission.

U.S. Department of Homeland Security, U.S. Customs and Border Protection, Office of Border Patrol. *Akwesasne Area Assessment FY2007.* Swanton, VT, 2007.

U.S. Department of Homeland Security, U.S. Customs and Border Protection, Office of Border Patrol. *Massena Station Threat Assessment FY 2012,* Massena, NY, 2012.

U.S. Department of Justice, Bureau of Alcohol, Tobacco, and Firearms. " Our Mission." Accessed 02 April 2013. http://www.atf.gov/content/About/about-atf.

U.S. Drug Enforcement Administration. "DEA Mission Statement." Accessed 26 March 2013. http://www.justice.gov/dea/about/mission.shtml.

U.S. Immigration and Customs Enforcement. "Border Security Enforcement Task Force." Accessed 26 March 2013. http://www.ice.gov/best/.

U.S. Immigration and Customs Enforcement. "Homeland Security Investigations." Accessed 27 March 2013. http://www.ice.gov/about/offices/homeland-security-investigations/.

U.S. Office of the Chairman of the Joint Chiefs of Staff. *Doctrine for the Armed Forces of the United States.* Joint Publication (JP) 1. Washington, DC: CJCS, 20 March 2007.

U.S. Office of the Chairman of the Joint Chiefs of Staff. *Joint Operations.* Joint Publication (JP) 3-0. Washington, DC: CJCS, 11 August 2011.

Vego, Milan. *Joint Operational Warfare Theory and Practice.* Newport, RI: U.S. Naval War College, 2007.

Von Hlatky, Stefanie "The Rhetoric and Reality of Border Policy Coordination Between Canada and the U.S." *International Journal* 67, no. 2 (2012) 437-443. http://internationaljournal.ca/post/26182981113/volume-67-issue-2-a-new-agenda-for-peace.

Washington Post, Politics. "Homeland Security Department." Accessed 30, March 2013.http://www.washingtonpost.com/politics/homeland-security department/gIQALxPx4O_topic.html

www.ingramcontent.com/pod-product-compliance
Lightning Source LLC
Chambersburg PA
CBHW060813290526
45792CB00005BA/1633